D0016614

CONTENTS

Revised Edition

© LADYBIRD BOOKS LTD MCMLXXXI

HOW IT WORKS...
THE AEROPLANE

by DAVID CAREY

with illustrations by
B H ROBINSON
and GERALD WITCOMB MSIAD

Ladybird Books Loughborough

Introduction

Of the three modes of travel, by land, water or air, air travel has always presented the greatest problem. It is only in fairly recent years that man has been able to build a really reliable machine to transport him efficiently and safely in the air. That machine is, of course, the aeroplane, and it is the purpose of this book to describe as simply as possible how and why an aeroplane works.

Motor cars travel on solid ground and have only to be propelled along. Boats and ships are supported by the water and will remain afloat under all normal conditions. But an aeroplane is heavier than the air in which it has to fly, yet it must be got off the ground, made to stay in the air in spite of its weight and finally brought back to earth gently without damage.

To discover how an aeroplane works, we must first find out about the air itself, how it behaves and how it affects an object moving through it. The way an aeroplane is built to make use of the air is important, as is also the method by which it is controlled and made to obey the wishes of the pilot.

It is a big subject but a truly fascinating one.

The air

There is a huge envelope of air around the surface of the earth. This air has an *atmospheric pressure* due to the weight of all the air above it. As we leave the earth's surface and go higher, the pressure becomes less because there is less air above to press down. At sea level the air pressure is nearly fifteen pounds on every square inch of surface; at twenty thousand feet this reduces to seven pounds to the square inch; at sixty thousand feet the air pressure is only one pound per square inch.

Air is also *compressible*, which means that it is more compressed, or denser nearer the ground. Once again, this is because of the pressure of all the air above. Because it is more dense, air at sea level is heavier than the air higher up. If we use the same height examples as before, we find that one hundred cubic feet of air weighs nearly eight pounds at sea level, only four pounds at twenty thousand feet and less than three-quarters of a pound at sixty thousand feet.

These differences of air pressure and density have a very great bearing on the design of aeroplanes, a fact you will be able to understand better as you read further into this book.

PRESSURE

WEIGHT

100 cu. ft.

1 SQ. INCH

AT 60,000 FEET

100 cu. ft.

1 SQ. INCH

AT 20,000 FEET

15lb

100 cu. ft.

1 SQ. INCH

AT SEA LEVEL

Lift and drag

To enable an aeroplane to fly in the air it must be given a lifting force at least equal to its own weight. How is this lift to be provided? Let us first consider a more simple flying object – a kite. The strings of a kite are so fitted that when the kite is flown it is not flat or upright but inclined at an angle, the front or *leading edge* being higher than the rear or *trailing edge*. Have you ever noticed this? The angle at which the kite is inclined is known as the *angle of attack*.

As you give the kite speed by holding the string and running, it will rise into the air and if you pay out the string it will rise higher and higher. The upward force which makes the kite rise is called the *lift*. If you grip the string tightly and draw the kite toward you in the air, you will feel a pull as the air tries to hold it back. This pull is known as *drag* and it acts against the direction of flight.

With aeroplanes, lift is a useful force which is essential to flight. It is obtained partly by the wings and partly by the aeroplane's forward speed. Drag is a backward pull which hinders forward motion and has to be reduced to a minimum.

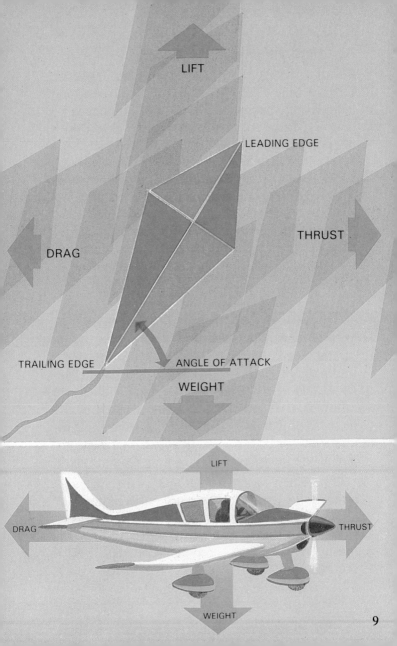

LIFT

LEADING EDGE

THRUST

DRAG

TRAILING EDGE

ANGLE OF ATTACK

WEIGHT

LIFT

DRAG

THRUST

WEIGHT

9

Aeroplane wings

So far we have been dealing with the simplest form of wing – the kite – with its flat surfaces and light weight. Aeroplanes need something much more efficient, and designers have developed wings of special, curved shape known as *aerofoils*. An aerofoil is really made up of two surfaces, an upper and a lower, each with a different curve or *camber*. There are two main reasons for this: firstly, a curved surface gives better lift, as explained overleaf, and secondly, an aeroplane wing has to get a heavy machine off the ground, so it must have thickness into which the necessary strength can be built.

In the previous chapter we mentioned the angle at which the kite was inclined upward, that is, the angle of attack. Aeroplane wings also have an angle of attack and are fitted to the fuselage with the leading edge slightly higher than the trailing edge when seen in the flying position. An increased angle of attack gives more lift, as with the kite, but also increases the drag. For normal flight the angle of attack has to be just right to ensure sufficient lift and at the same time cause as little drag as possible.

On modern fast-flying aeroplanes the angle of attack is very small, usually not much more than about two degrees from the horizontal when in level flight. With this small angle of attack the aeroplane must travel at a high speed before it will lift off the ground.

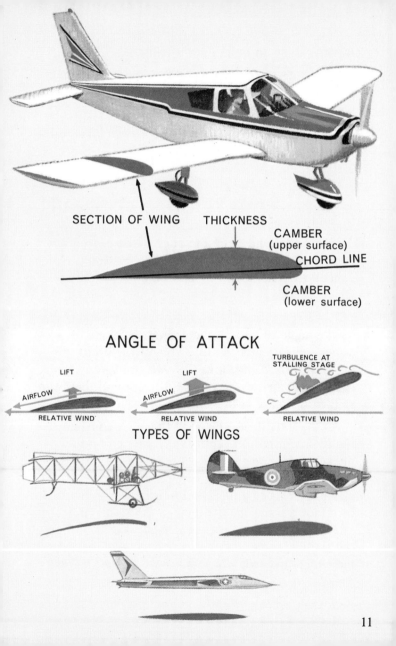

SECTION OF WING   THICKNESS

CAMBER
(upper surface)

CHORD LINE

CAMBER
(lower surface)

ANGLE OF ATTACK

LIFT

AIRFLOW

RELATIVE WIND

LIFT

AIRFLOW

RELATIVE WIND

TURBULENCE AT
STALLING STAGE

RELATIVE WIND

TYPES OF WINGS

Airflow over an aeroplane's wing

For an aeroplane's wing to give the lift required for flight, the general airflow over and around the wing must be streamlined and not turbulent.

The amount of lift the wings give will depend on:
1 their shape;
2 their area;
3 the density of the air through which they fly;
4 the speed at which the air passes over them;
5 the angle of attack.

Numbers 4 and 5 are the ones which can be controlled by the pilot, although he has some control over number 3 by choosing the height at which he flies.

For a given speed, the amount of lift is controlled by the angle of attack, the greater the angle of attack – the greater the lift. This is true up to the angle of attack known as the *stalling angle*, when the general airflow becomes turbulent and there is a sudden decrease in the amount of lift.

As the weight of a plane in the air is constant, the lift required to keep it flying straight and level must also be constant. Because of this, a test pilot can, at a safe height, fly straight and level, gradually reducing his speed but increasing his angle of attack so that the lift remains constant, until the stalling angle is reached. In straight and level flight, the stalling angle will always be reached at the same indicated airspeed, which is known as the *stalling speed*.

STREAMLINED AIRFLOW PAST A WING IN SLOW FLIGHT

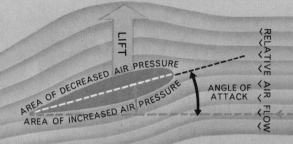

LIFT

AREA OF DECREASED AIR PRESSURE

AREA OF INCREASED AIR PRESSURE

ANGLE OF ATTACK

RELATIVE AIR FLOW

The airflow remains streamlined until the stalling angle is reached, when the airflow quite suddenly becomes turbulent, resulting in a sudden decrease in lift.

Any attempt to increase further the angle of attack will result in even more loss of lift.

TURBULENT AIRFLOW PAST A WING AT STALLING ANGLE

LIFT

TURBULENCE

INCREASED ANGLE OF ATTACK

RELATIVE AIR FLOW

Forces acting on an aeroplane

We can now sum up the various forces which act on an aeroplane and see how they affect the whole machine in straight and level flight.

An aeroplane gains almost all its lift from the wings, the remaining parts help very little. On the other hand it is the body, or fuselage, engine mountings and other protruding portions which cause most of the drag. We must therefore have all these parts as smooth and streamlined as possible. A dart will fly better than a ball because it creates less drag, so aircraft designers must try to achieve a dart shape.

Lift on an aeroplane acts vertically upward, the machine's weight pushes vertically downward. To fly straight and level, the lift must equal the weight. If the lift were greater the aeroplane would go higher and higher. If the weight were greater the machine would get lower and lower until it hit the ground.

Then there are the horizontal forces; *drag*, which as we now know, is a backward force holding the aeroplane back, and *thrust* which is the forward pull provided by the engines. Just as lift and weight are equal for straight and level flight, so the thrust must also equal the total drag. So long as thrust is greater than drag, the aeroplane will increase its speed.

FORCES ACTING ON AN AEROPLANE

LIFT

DRAG

THRUST

WEIGHT

Stability and movements of an aeroplane

Another matter which greatly concerns designers of aeroplanes is *stability*. This can be described briefly as the way an aeroplane itself corrects unwanted movements caused by air disturbances, without the pilot having to adjust his controls. There are three kinds of movement which the aeroplane's natural stability is designed to correct.

1 PITCHING: This is a movement in which the nose of the aeroplane is forced up or down by some disturbance of the air. An aeroplane must have *longitudinal stability* to bring the nose back to its original level position. The tail plane is the part fitted to do this job.

2 ROLLING: An aeroplane rolls when the wing tips are forced up or down. In this movement the machine is likely to sideslip in the direction of the lower wing tip unless it is corrected by the *lateral stability*. Lateral stability is usually obtained by inclining the wings slightly upward from the fuselage to wing tip when the aeroplane is made. The angle at which the wings are set is known as the *dihedral angle* and is not adjustable.

3 YAWING: This is a turning movement in which the nose tends to turn left or right and the aeroplane tries to fly sideways. The tail fin is fitted to provide *directional stability* and keep the aeroplane in its proper straight ahead position.

PITCHING

TAIL PLANE

LONGITUDINAL STABILITY

ROLLING

DIHEDRAL ANGLE

LATERAL STABILITY

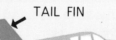

TAIL FIN

YAWING

DIRECTIONAL STABILITY

Controlling the aeroplane

However stable an aeroplane may be, the pilot must be able to control it; to increase or decrease height and to change direction whenever necessary.

LONGITUDINAL CONTROL raises or lowers the nose of the aeroplane and is provided by *elevators* at the rear of the tail plane. Forward movement of the pilot's control column lowers the elevators. This increases the upward force on the tail, causes the nose to tilt downward and the aeroplane to descend. The operation is reversed to raise the nose and climb.

LATERAL CONTROL is obtained by the pilot moving the control column sideways (or by turning a half-wheel at the top of the column). This operates *ailerons* at the rear of each wing, near the tip. Movement of the column to the *right* lowers the *left-hand* aileron, increases the lift on the *left-hand* wing and banks the aeroplane to the *right*. At the same time, the *right-hand* aileron has been raised to reduce the lift on the *right-hand* wing and so lower the *right-hand* wing. In the picture this is shown looking at the tail of the aeroplane.

DIRECTIONAL CONTROL is effected by means of a rudder on the tail fin, worked by the pilot's feet. Pressing the left pedal down turns the rudder to the left, increases the force on the left of the tail fin and pushes the aeroplane's nose to the left.

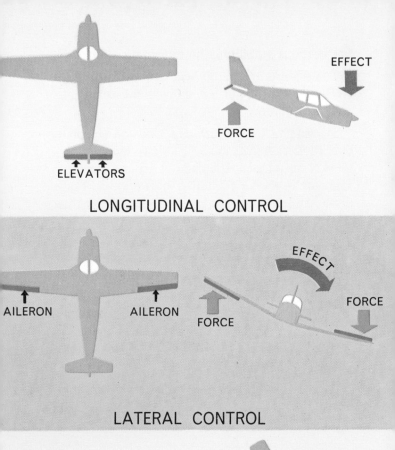

LONGITUDINAL CONTROL

EFFECT

FORCE

ELEVATORS

LATERAL CONTROL

AILERON

AILERON

EFFECT

FORCE

FORCE

DIRECTIONAL CONTROL

RUDDER

FORCE

EFFECT

19

More about stability — the automatic pilot

The feature of stability was dealt with on page 16, but it is an important subject and worth enlarging upon.

Stability varies for different kinds of aeroplanes. Fast fighter aircraft must be able to manoeuvre quickly onto an enemy plane or ground target. They are in the air for fairly short periods. For these reasons they have less built-in stability than larger machines and more direct pilot control. It would be a very poor fighter aircraft which automatically went back to its original position every time a pilot tried to manoeuvre it.

On the other hand, large air liners which fly steadily from one point to another for several hours

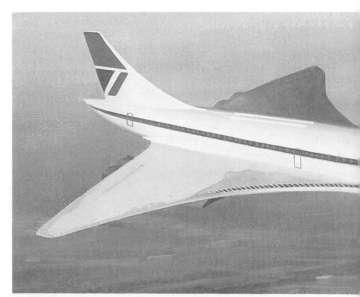

at a time need a greater degree of built-in stability so that the pilot does not have to keep adjusting his controls for every little movement of the aeroplane. This would be very tiring, for instance, on a flight across the Atlantic. To help the pilot still further, and give even greater stability, most commercial aeroplanes are fitted with an *automatic pilot*, sometimes known as 'George'. This is a system of gyroscopes and electronic devices which keeps the flying controls in the right positions for straight and level flight. The pilot can switch to 'George' when he wishes to rest or move about the aircraft.

Air speed and ground speed

There is another aspect of flying we must now know about, that is *flying speeds*. There are, in fact, two kinds of speed: the *ground speed*, which is the actual speed of the aeroplane in relation to the ground, and the *air speed*, which is the speed relative to the air. These are two quite different things.

Let us go back to the kite for a moment. If, in *still air*, you run with a kite at five miles per hour, its *ground speed* will be five miles per hour because that is the actual speed at which you are pulling it over the ground. Now, suppose you are running at five miles per hour against a light breeze of five miles per hour. The *ground speed* will still be the same but, because the air is passing the kite at ten miles per hour, the *air speed* of the kite will be ten miles per hour; that is, the speed at which you are running *plus* the speed of the air blowing past the kite. Stand still with your kite in the same breeze. Its *ground speed* is now nothing, but the air is passing the kite at five miles per hour, so its *air speed* is five miles per hour.

Ground speed decides how long an aeroplane will take to fly from one place to another. Air speed provides the lifting force and the drag. Your kite will remain in the air in a good breeze even if you stand still, and you will still feel the drag on the string.

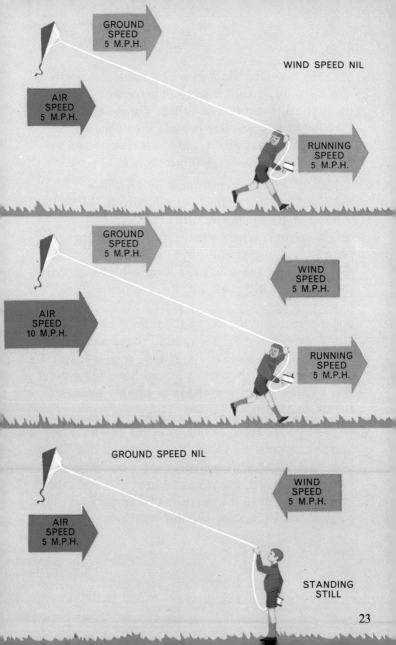

GROUND SPEED 5 M.P.H.

WIND SPEED NIL

AIR SPEED 5 M.P.H.

RUNNING SPEED 5 M.P.H.

GROUND SPEED 5 M.P.H.

WIND SPEED 5 M.P.H.

AIR SPEED 10 M.P.H.

RUNNING SPEED 5 M.P.H.

GROUND SPEED NIL

WIND SPEED 5 M.P.H.

AIR SPEED 5 M.P.H.

STANDING STILL

Taking off

In the previous chapters we have learnt something about the air, how it affects an aeroplane and how the aeroplane can be controlled. These have been very important chapters because they concern the basic principles of flight. Now it is time to see how an aeroplane actually gets into the air.

First of all the aircraft must be correctly positioned on the airfield, so it is 'driven' along the ground under the power of its engines. This is called *taxying*. When it reaches the end of the runway it is turned into the wind, that is, toward the direction from which the wind is blowing. With the wind blowing toward it, the aeroplane already has a little air speed. The throttles are opened, the engines roar and the aeroplane rapidly gains speed along the runway. As the ground speed increases so does the air speed, until the *flying speed* is reached. At that moment the aeroplane can leave the ground and become airborne if the pilot *slightly* increases the angle of attack.

The upward force of the air acting on the wings, and the aeroplane's speed, have provided the necessary lift to start it flying. After safety speed has been reached, the pilot can then ease back the control column to lift the nose of the machine further and so increase the rate of climb.

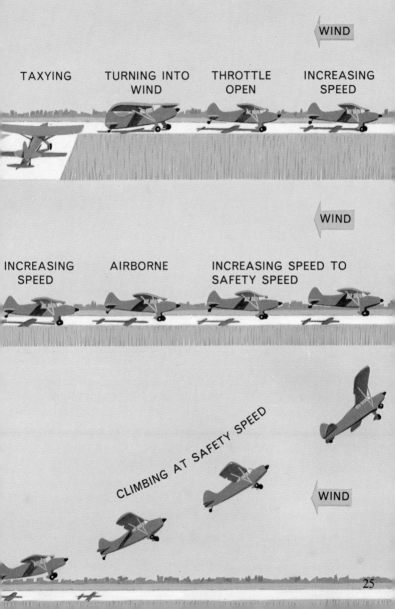

WIND

TAXYING   TURNING INTO WIND   THROTTLE OPEN   INCREASING SPEED

WIND

INCREASING SPEED   AIRBORNE   INCREASING SPEED TO SAFETY SPEED

CLIMBING AT SAFETY SPEED

WIND

25

Level flight and the speed range

For straight and level flight, lift must always equal weight. Lift is controlled by the angle of attack and by speed. If the pilot of an aeroplane increases his speed, and does not alter his angle of attack (see pages 12 and 13) the aeroplane will rise. Therefore, to maintain level flight, he must push the control column forward to lower the nose and so decrease the angle of attack. This restores the lift/weight balance.

On the other hand, if the pilot reduces speed without altering his angle of attack he will lose height. He must therefore pull the control column back and increase the angle of attack to keep his aeroplane in level flight.

The pilot of an aeroplane may wish to fly as fast as possible; he may wish to fly at the most economical cruising speed to conserve fuel or he may wish to fly as slowly as possible at the instant of landing. Aeroplanes are designed to fly at certain speeds and at certain heights. There is a maximum speed beyond which the power of the engines will not take them. There is also a minimum flying speed below which an aeroplane will not leave the ground: if it is already in the air it will stall and crash. This is because the speed is too low to maintain sufficient lift even when the angle of attack is greatly increased. This is known as the *stalling speed*.

EFFECT OF INCREASED SPEED

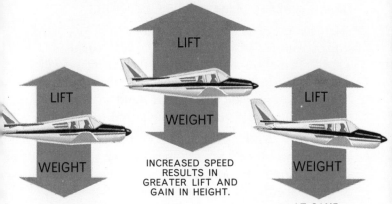

LIFT

WEIGHT

STEADY SPEED

LIFT

WEIGHT

INCREASED SPEED
RESULTS IN
GREATER LIFT AND
GAIN IN HEIGHT.

LIFT

WEIGHT

AT SAME
INCREASED SPEED,
A *DECREASED* ANGLE
OF ATTACK IS
NECESSARY TO
MAINTAIN SAME
HEIGHT.

EFFECT OF REDUCED SPEED

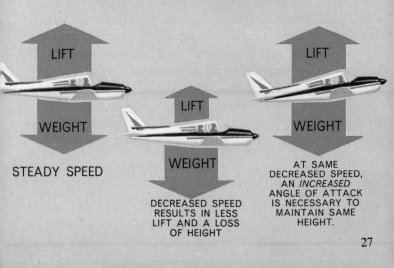

LIFT

WEIGHT

STEADY SPEED

LIFT

WEIGHT

DECREASED SPEED
RESULTS IN LESS
LIFT AND A LOSS
OF HEIGHT

LIFT

WEIGHT

AT SAME
DECREASED SPEED,
AN *INCREASED*
ANGLE OF ATTACK
IS NECESSARY TO
MAINTAIN SAME
HEIGHT.

How a climbing plane reaches its ceiling

On the previous page it was shown that for straight and level flight, lift must always equal weight. If the lift is greater, then the aeroplane will rise. It follows that an aeroplane can climb if it has the power to provide more speed – and so more lift – than that required for straight and level flight.

In theory, all the pilot has to do is increase speed or lift the machine's nose to increase the angle of attack, or both. In practice it is not so easy because of the properties of air which were mentioned at the beginning of the book. As the aeroplane climbs higher, the density of the air becomes less. This means less lift at a given true air speed, which means that more power is needed to increase the true air speed if the angle of attack is to remain the same. If the angle of attack is increased, more power is needed to overcome the extra drag.

The higher an aeroplane flies, the worse is this effect. Unfortunately, with piston-engined aircraft the less dense air also has an effect on the engine, so that the power available also decreases with height. When all the power available is only maintaining straight and level flight at the best angle of attack, the aeroplane is at its *ceiling*. With jet engines, however, the less dense air does not have such a serious effect on the power available.

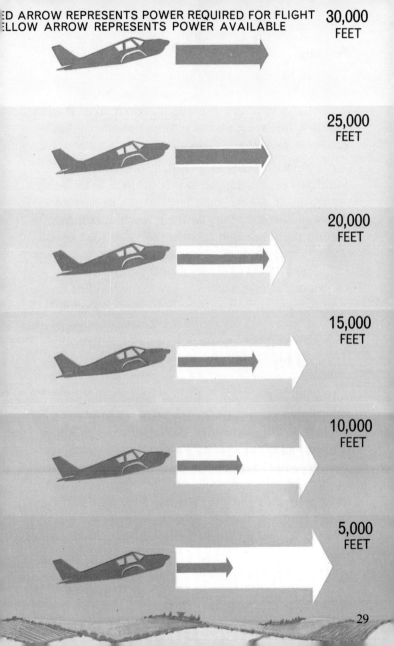

ED ARROW REPRESENTS POWER REQUIRED FOR FLIGHT
ELLOW ARROW REPRESENTS POWER AVAILABLE

30,000 FEET

25,000 FEET

20,000 FEET

15,000 FEET

10,000 FEET

5,000 FEET

29

Turning

If you have ever flown in an aeroplane or watched from the ground, you will have noticed that whenever a turn is made it is done in a slanting position, one wing tip lower than the other. This is known as *banking*.

An object moving in a straight line tries to continue on that line when it is turned. A car being driven round a bend on a level road will only go round the bend so long as the tyres maintain their grip on the road. If it is driven too fast the car will skid towards its original line of travel due to a force acting away from the centre of the turn. This is known as the *centrifugal force*. If the bend in the road is built up on the outside to form a sloping bank, the car will go round more easily and at a higher speed because the weight and centrifugal force combined will then act at right-angles to the slope.

If a pilot tries to turn his aeroplane without banking, it will tend to move sideways in its original line of flight, like the car in a skid. When banked and turned by the combined use of rudder, ailerons and elevators, the wings provide extra lift against the outward force and allow the aeroplane to turn smoothly in the required direction, because all the forces acting on the aeroplane are in balance.

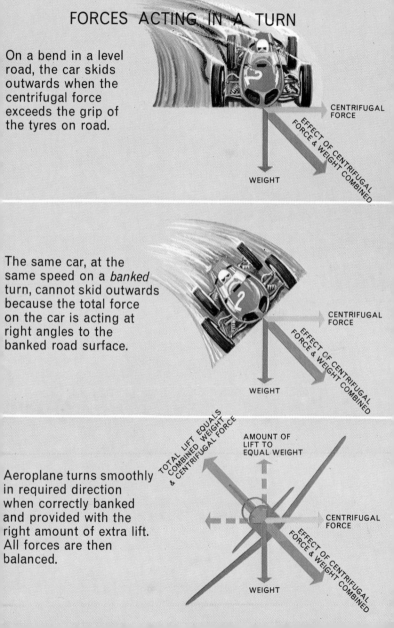

FORCES ACTING IN A TURN

On a bend in a level road, the car skids outwards when the centrifugal force exceeds the grip of the tyres on road.

CENTRIFUGAL FORCE

EFFECT OF CENTRIFUGAL FORCE & WEIGHT COMBINED

WEIGHT

The same car, at the same speed on a *banked* turn, cannot skid outwards because the total force on the car is acting at right angles to the banked road surface.

CENTRIFUGAL FORCE

EFFECT OF CENTRIFUGAL FORCE & WEIGHT COMBINED

WEIGHT

Aeroplane turns smoothly in required direction when correctly banked and provided with the right amount of extra lift. All forces are then balanced.

TOTAL LIFT EQUALS COMBINED WEIGHT & CENTRIFUGAL FORCE

AMOUNT OF LIFT TO EQUAL WEIGHT

CENTRIFUGAL FORCE

EFFECT OF CENTRIFUGAL FORCE & WEIGHT COMBINED

WEIGHT

Landing

Landing an aeroplane, that is, transferring it from the air to the ground as gently as possible, is perhaps the most difficult manoeuvre of flying. It demands flying the aeroplane as slowly as possible without stalling, which in itself requires considerable skill on the part of the pilot.

When approaching the ground, an aeroplane has both forward and downward speed. The forward speed (in relation to the ground) which has been progressively decreased by cutting the engine power, is still further reduced by landing into the wind whenever possible, but runway positions on modern airports do not always allow this to be done exactly and cross-wind landings sometimes take place.

At a point close to the ground, forward speed in relation to the air is reduced by completely closing the throttle. As the speed falls off (because the pilot has stopped all thrust but cannot reduce the drag), lift is maintained by raising the aircraft's nose slightly and progressively, thus increasing the angle of attack, and so keeping lift equal to the weight as the speed falls to its minimum for flying. Finally, as the forward speed continues to fall, a condition is reached when the aeroplane is no longer moving at its flying speed. Ideally, this occurs at the moment when the wheels of the undercarriage touch the runway and the weight of the aeroplane is transferred smoothly from the air to the ground.

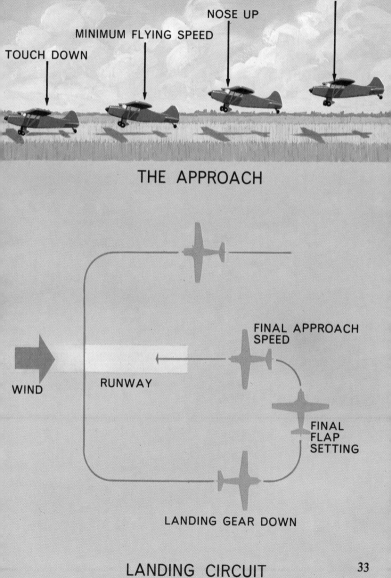

TOUCH DOWN

MINIMUM FLYING SPEED

NOSE UP

CLOSE THROTTLE

THE APPROACH

WIND

RUNWAY

FINAL APPROACH
SPEED

FINAL
FLAP
SETTING

LANDING GEAR DOWN

LANDING CIRCUIT

Reduction of landing speeds

Landing speeds should be kept as low as possible, yet the aeroplane must be capable of a good turn of speed for normal flight. It is important that the lift of the wings equals the weight of the machine until the moment of landing. Because the landing speed needs to be kept down to a minimum, extra lift is required from the wings. How can this be obtained? By a greater angle of attack? The pilot can provide this by lifting the nose, but it is a relatively small movement otherwise the aeroplane might stall. By more camber on the wings? By greater wing area? Both these would help a great deal but bigger wings with more camber create more drag and would slow down the aeroplane during normal flight.

Aeroplane designers have found a means of overcoming this problem by the use of *flaps*. These are usually hinged at the trailing edge of the wings. During the landing operation the pilot moves a control which causes the flaps to move out from the wings in a downward direction. This, in effect, especially in the case of the extension flap, forms a curved extension of the wings to increase their camber and area and provide enough extra lift to lower the stalling speed appreciably.

During normal flight the flaps are tucked up into the wings and flying speeds are not affected.

SIMPLE or CAMBER FLAP

SPLIT FLAP

EXTENSION or FOWLER FLAP

The propeller

In piston-engined and propeller-turbine aeroplanes, the propeller is used to provide the thrust which gives the plane its forward speed.

The blades of a propeller are not flat but curved like an aerofoil, and behave like an aerofoil. They are also set at an angle to the direction of rotation. As the propeller rotates, the blades strike the air at an angle of attack and develop *thrust* in just the same way that a wing develops lift. Imagine turning a nut on the thread of a bolt. For each complete turn the nut is carried forward along the bolt. Similarly the 'pitch', or angle of a propeller's blades, decides the distance the propeller moves forward through the air in one revolution. The faster an aeroplane is designed to fly, the coarser the pitch so that the propeller goes forward the greatest possible distance during each revolution.

Modern commercial aeroplanes are usually fitted with variable and reversible pitch propellers, and the pitch angle can be varied by the pilot to suit flying conditions. A fine pitch (smaller angle) is required for take-off, to give maximum thrust at low forward speeds and high revolutions, and a coarse pitch (larger angle) to maintain thrust at high speeds and reduced engine revolutions when cruising. Reverse pitch completely reverses the action of the propeller so that instead of pulling the aircraft forward, it pushes it back. This is used after landing to slow down the aircraft quickly.

ADVANCE PER REVOLUTION

FINE PITCH

for maximum thrust at slow forward speeds and high revolutions.

COARSE PITCH

for thrust at high forward speeds and reduced revolutions.

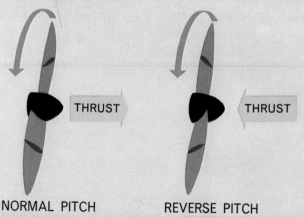

NORMAL PITCH

REVERSE PITCH

Piston engines

In a book of this kind it is not possible to discuss in detail how the different types of engines work. All that can be done is to indicate the various engines in use and what are their basic differences.

Piston engines operate on the same principle as those in an ordinary motor car*. That is to say, they run on petrol and have pistons which move up and down in cylinders. These rotate a crankshaft which provides the drive. In the case of an aeroplane, the part being driven is the propeller.

There are two main types of piston engine: one has the pistons and cylinders arranged in line as in the normal motor car. However, as the power is increased and more cylinders are used, this basic arrangement is varied. The cylinders can then be mounted in blocks in the shape of a V, X or H. The second type is the radial engine in which the cylinders radiate outward from the centre and have a circular appearance when viewed from the front.

When piston engines are used for aircraft propulsion, it is the radial type that is fitted on most multi-engined commercial aeroplanes. In-line engines are more common on smaller single-engined machines.

*see 'How it works – The Motor Car'.

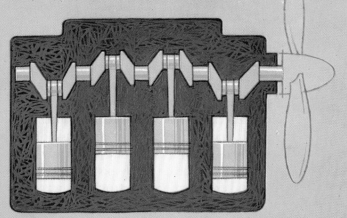

IN LINE

V

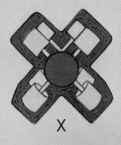

X

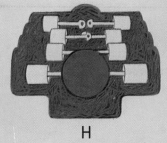

H

RADIAL

39

Jets and propeller turbines

New commercial aeroplanes are designed for use with gas turbine, or jet, engines. The piston-operated petrol engine is no longer efficient enough for modern applications and has been replaced. The aircraft gas turbine is more reliable and runs longer between overhauls. It produces continuous power instead of the typical 'beat' of the piston engine. Its fuel (kerosene) is cheaper than petrol; it is lighter and better shaped to minimise drag and vibration.

Briefly, the operation of a turbine engine is as follows: air is sucked into the front of the engine by a rotating compressor, then forced into combustion chambers into which the kerosene is sprayed and burnt. The tremendous heat thus generated expands the main volume of air which moves at great speed through flame tubes on to the blades of the turbine wheels. This causes the wheels to rotate and so power is produced, which drives the compressor and, by a system of gears, turns the propeller. In the case of a turbo-jet engine, the heated air only drives the compressor then comes out of the exhaust tail pipe as a jet and the aeroplane is forced forward.

The turbo-prop engine works best at slow speeds (up to 400mph) and the turbo-jet works best at very high speeds (as in the supersonic *Concorde*). If the two types of engines are combined, a turbo-fan engine is produced which works well at both high and low speeds.

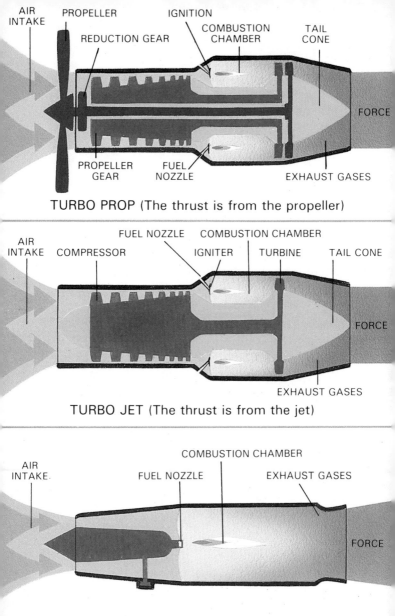

TURBO PROP (The thrust is from the propeller)

TURBO JET (The thrust is from the jet)

RAM JET (The thrust is from the jet)

41

Flight instruments

Although the working of an aeroplane depends to a large extent on the properties of the air in which it flies, and on the design of the aeroplane to make use of these properties, the pilot has a great responsibility in actually flying the machine. The flight deck of an air liner is an awesome sight to the novice, with all its instruments, dials, controls, switches and indicator lights which tell the pilot every detail of what is happening in every part of the aeroplane. There are so many of them that we can only mention a few.

There is an *air speed indicator*. This is connected to the tube you can sometimes see protruding forward from the nose or wing of an aeroplane. An *altimeter* gives the altitude or height above ground. A *compass* indicates direction and enables a course to be set. An *artificial horizon* shows whether the aeroplane is flying level, without pitch or roll: this is most important for blind flying at night or in cloud when the pilot cannot see the ground. A *turn and side-slip indicator* shows the pilot that he has the right amount of rudder and aileron movement, and his rate of turn. A *rate of climb indicator* shows the rate of ascent and descent. And there are a great many other instruments, as you can see in the picture opposite.

Navigation

To get an aeroplane into the air and fly it is one problem; to fly it in the right direction and land at a point hundreds, perhaps thousands, of miles away presents another set of problems altogether. The process of finding the way from one place to another is known as navigation and, so far as aeroplanes are concerned, this frequently has to be done at night, or in cloudy weather, when the ground cannot be seen.

The basic aircraft instruments used for navigation, namely the airspeed indicator, the magnetic compass and an accurate clock, only give information about what the aircraft is doing in relation to the air through which it is flying. But unless the day is windless, the air as a whole is itself moving in relation to the ground, so the navigator must calculate what allowances must be made for the action of the wind on the plane at the height at which he is flying.

Modern airliners have other navigational aids. Radar allows a pilot to 'see' through the darkness or clouds, and radio direction-finding equipment can be tuned-in to ground stations so that the aeroplane's position can be accurately pin-pointed. Of course, on a clear day when the ground is visible, navigation becomes a fairly simple matter of locating landmarks, such as towns and rivers, which can be easily recognised.

SHOWING HOW A PLANE IS BLOWN OFF COURSE BY WIND (If speed and direction of wind is not allowed for)

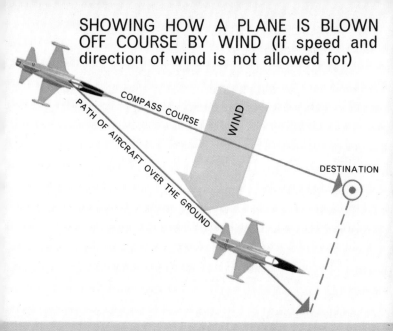

CORRECT COURSE ALLOWING FOR DIRECTION AND SPEED OF WIND

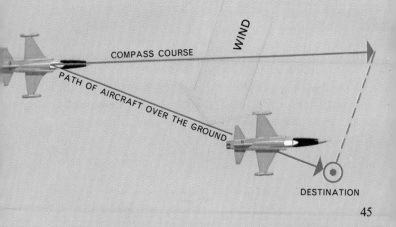

Auxiliary equipment

Modern aeroplanes are very complicated machines carrying a great mass of equipment, all of which must work properly. Perhaps the most obvious item of auxiliary equipment is the undercarriage which carries the wheels. The undercarriage is very useful on the ground but as soon as the aeroplane is in the air it becomes a nuisance. Hanging below the aircraft it would get in the way of the air flow, cause drag and reduce both lift and speed. That is why the undercarriage is always *retracted* into the wings as soon as the wheels leave the ground. Watch for yourself next time you see an aeroplane take off. The retracting machinery is controlled by the pilot and acts electrically or hydraulically.

On larger aeroplanes the flying controls are also power-operated. The pilot's hands or feet moving the control column, or rudder bar, set a hydraulic system in motion which in turn moves the ailerons, elevators or rudder. To have to do this without power-assistance would be very hard work, if it were possible at all.

Electricity is needed to operate the lights and to work the radar and radio systems. Power for all this and other equipment is often provided by the main engines, but on some large aeroplanes, small auxiliary engines are fitted to deal with the extra power loads.

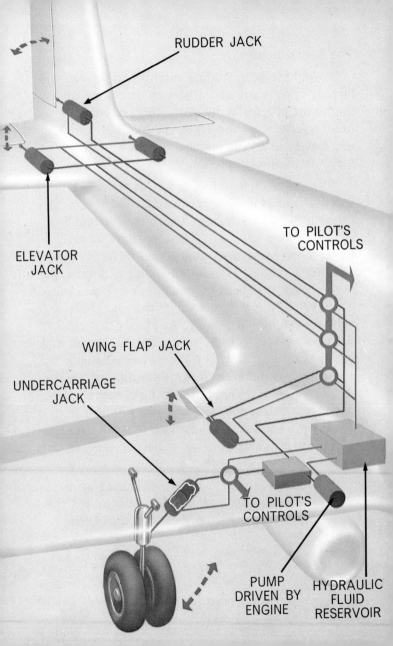

RUDDER JACK

ELEVATOR
JACK

TO PILOT'S
CONTROLS

WING FLAP JACK

UNDERCARRIAGE
JACK

TO PILOT'S
CONTROLS

PUMP
DRIVEN BY
ENGINE

HYDRAULIC
FLUID
RESERVOIR

The sound barrier

If you have been reading carefully so far you will already know more about how an aeroplane works than most people. Many aeroplanes, especially military ones, can now fly at the speed of sound, and faster, so a little information on what this means is of special interest.

When an aeroplane flies at speeds below the speed of sound, pressures caused by its movement through the air are transmitted to the surrounding air in the form of waves. These pressure waves travel at the same speed that sound travels in the air, that is, about seven hundred and sixty miles per hour. Below the speed of sound an aeroplane will travel behind the pressure waves and sound waves, and you can hear it coming. At exactly the speed of sound, it travels with the waves and the sound, and you will not hear it until it passes immediately above you. If it travels towards you faster than the speed of sound, it flies through the pressure waves, passes you before they do, and you will hear it coming after it has gone! Passing through the sound waves is often known as passing through the *sound barrier*.

Sonic bangs are the shock waves caused by an aeroplane flying faster than sound. Planes that can travel faster than the speed of sound are called supersonic.

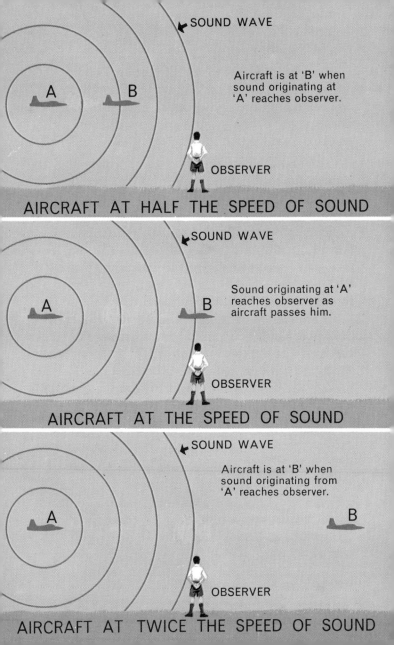

SOUND WAVE

A   B

Aircraft is at 'B' when sound originating at 'A' reaches observer.

OBSERVER

AIRCRAFT AT HALF THE SPEED OF SOUND

SOUND WAVE

A   B

Sound originating at 'A' reaches observer as aircraft passes him.

OBSERVER

AIRCRAFT AT THE SPEED OF SOUND

SOUND WAVE

A   B

Aircraft is at 'B' when sound originating from 'A' reaches observer.

OBSERVER

AIRCRAFT AT TWICE THE SPEED OF SOUND

The helicopter

The helicopter is used for all purposes where proper landing fields are not available, and it is often in the news carrying out difficult acts of rescue, transporting troops and supplies, even plucking astronauts from the sea.

Vertical lift is provided by rotating wings, or blades of aerofoil shape, on top of the aircraft. The blades are set at an angle and provide upward thrust in the same way that a normal aeroplane propeller provides forward thrust. By forcing air downward, they lift the helicopter upward; the faster the speed of rotation the greater the lift. Once the machine has gained height, the whole rotor system is tilted slightly forward. At this angle there is a combined upward and forward thrust. This gives the helicopter its forward speed as well as sufficient lift to maintain height. The little propeller which spins round at the side of the tail is to prevent the helicopter from rotating in the opposite direction to the rotor, and acts as a rudder.

Hovering over one spot is done by selecting the correct speed and setting of the rotor blades so that their vertical lift is exactly equal to the weight of the machine.

Some jet aircraft can also hover and lift vertically if the exhaust gases from the jet engine are directed downwards as well as being used to drive the aircraft forward.

Index